THE *Nature* OF *Excellence*

"Look deep into nature, and then you will understand everything better."

ALBERT EINSTEIN

THE NATURE OF EXCELLENCE

Text Copyright © 2008 by David Cottrell and Lee J. Colan
Photography Copyright © 2008 by Tom Fox

Printed in China
ISBN 978-0-9798009-4-8

All photographs in this book are available as fine art prints.
Visit www.TomFoxPhotography.com
or call 901-753-8252.

Watch a three-minute inspirational video featuring the words and images from
The Nature of Excellence at www.CornerStoneLeadership.com.

Most of the photographs featured in this book are available as inspirational note cards,
posters and desktop prints. Customized gift versions of this book are also available.

Visit **www.CornerStoneLeadership.com** or call 888-789-5323.

DEDICATION

To every person who has the passion, desire and willingness
to settle for nothing less than excellence.

*I*NTRODUCTION

THE *V*ALUES OF *E*XCELLENCE

THE *V*ISION OF *E*XCELLENCE

THE *A*CTS OF *E*XCELLENCE

$\mathcal{I}$NTRODUCTION

We are what we repeatedly do. Excellence, then, is not an act but a habit.

ARISTOTLE

Life's greatest lessons are learned from nature and from those who have lived before us. This book combines the stunning images of nature with quotations from successful people living in this and past generations.

The magnificent images in *The Nature of Excellence* were produced by natural lighting – no artificial lighting was used on any photograph in this book. Tom Fox is passionate about his photography, and each image reflects that passion as well as Tom's love for capturing nature at its best.

The quotes are a collection of David Cottrell and Lee Colan's favorites. The wisdom of successful pioneers from all sectors of business, industry, science and education provides an opportunity for us to learn from the past, understand the present, and prepare for the future. Each quote was carefully selected to inspire, motivate and encourage.

May the timeless wisdom in this book accelerate your journey toward excellence!

THE VALUES OF EXCELLENCE

Character is the foundation upon which we must build to win respect.

Just as no worthy building can be erected on a weak foundation,

so no lasting reputation worthy of respect can be built on a weak character.

R.C. SAMSEL

INTEGRITY

COMMITMENT

PASSION

TRUTH

COURAGE

TEAMWORK

$\mathcal{I}$NTEGRITY

Without a doubt, your personal integrity is your most prized possession. Each day, that integrity is constantly tested, and you have an opportunity to prove it or lose it with every decision you make.

Doing the right thing is not always the easiest thing – but it is always the right thing to do. Choosing to do the right thing – even when it's painful – ensures you will maintain your most precious possession throughout your personal and professional journey.

I got up before sunrise to photograph this solitary cypress tree in the fog.
In the predawn stillness, the sky and water magically blend together.

TOM FOX

REELFOOT LAKE STATE PARK – TENNESSEE

Integrity is never being ashamed of your reflection.

integrity

There is no pillow as soft as a clear conscience.

JOHN WOODEN

The time is always right to do what is right.

MARTIN LUTHER KING, JR.

A good name is more desirable than great riches;
to be esteemed is better than silver or gold.

PROVERBS 22:1

What lies behind us and what lies before us
are tiny matters compared to what lies within us.

RALPH WALDO EMERSON

Until you make peace with who you are,
you'll never be content with what you have.

DORIS MORTMAN

It is better to be defeated on principle than to win on lies.

ARTHUR CALWELL

*Integrity is the commitment to do what is right regardless of the circumstances —
no hidden agendas, no political games. Do the right thing, period.*

KEN CARNES

It is no use walking anywhere to preach
unless our walking is our preaching.

ST. FRANCIS OF ASSISI

*In matters of style, swim with the current;
in matters of principle, stand like a rock.*

THOMAS JEFFERSON

*There can be no happiness if the things we believe in
are different from the things we do.*

FREYA STARK

COMMITMENT

It's easy to talk about commitment, but commitment is more than words. It's a choice, an attitude and a passion to achieve success, whatever the price.

Commitment is about doing what you say you'll do … when you say you'll do it. It's about under-promising or over-delivering. It's about being kind to yourself when you fall short … and it's about believing failure can mean being one step closer to success.

This pine tree tenaciously clings to a sandstone knob. Even amid its harsh environment, it has grown and remained vibrant. This tree reminds me to rise above my circumstances, live my life with tenacity and continue to grow.

TOM FOX

ZION NATIONAL PARK – UTAH

Winners are committed to 'hang in there' long enough to win.

When work, commitment and pleasure all become one and you reach
that deep well where passion lives, nothing is impossible.

ANONYMOUS

If a man is called to be a street sweeper, he should sweep streets
even as Michelangelo painted, or Beethoven composed music,
or Shakespeare wrote poetry. He should sweep streets so well
that all the hosts of heaven and earth will pause to say,
here lived a great street sweeper who did his job well.

MARTIN LUTHER KING, JR.

The world stands aside to let anyone
pass who knows where he is going.

DAVID STARR JORDAN

The tragedy of life doesn't lie in not reaching your goal.
The tragedy lies in having no goal to reach.

BENJAMIN MAYS

Standing in the middle of the road is very dangerous;
you get knocked down by traffic from both sides.

MARGARET THATCHER

There is one quality that one must possess to win,
and that is definiteness of purpose – the knowledge
of what one wants and a burning desire to possess it.

NAPOLEON HILL

There is no passion to be found in playing small –
in settling for a life that is less than what you are capable of living.

NELSON MANDELA

The quality of a person's life is in direct proportion
to their commitment to excellence,
regardless of their chosen field of endeavor.

VINCE LOMBARDI

If you want to be successful, know what you are doing,
love what you are doing and believe in what you are doing.

WILL ROGERS

Many men go fishing all of their lives
without knowing that it is not fish they are after.

HENRY DAVID THOREAU

$\mathscr{P}$ASSION

$\mathbf{H}$appiness comes from following your passion. Excellence comes from work that you are passionate about. Knowing what to do is certainly important, but knowing why you do it fuels your motivation … your passion. A strong passion enables you to find a way to achieve your goals … any goal. Passion turns your stumbling blocks into stepping stones. Not only does passion ignite your pursuit of excellence, passion also makes the journey more fun!

A violent storm engulfed the mountain region.
As dawn appeared, the storm broke, creating an amazing sunrise –
reminding me of the possibilities for new light, vision and opportunities.

Tom Fox

Great Smoky Mountains National Park – Tennessee

Passion exposes possibilities.

It's not enough to be busy. The question is, what are we busy about?

HENRY DAVID THOREAU

Empty pockets never held anyone back.
Only empty heads and empty hearts can do that.

NORMAN VINCENT PEALE

The more I want to get something done, the less I call it work.

RICHARD BACH

If you don't love what you do, you have two choices:
You can either change what you're doing, or you can change what you love.

BILLY COX

There is no passion to be found in playing small –
in settling for a life that is less than what you are capable of living.

NELSON MANDELA

Every man without passions has within him
no principle of action, nor motive to act.

CLAUDE A. HELVETIUS

Without passion man is a mere latent force and possibility,
like the flint which awaits the shock of the iron before it can give forth its spark.

HENRI-FREDERIC AMIEL

Life is not measured by the number of breaths we take,
but by the moments that take our breath away.

GEORGE CARLIN

Life is action and passion; therefore, it is required of a man that he should share
the passion and action of the time, at peril of being judged not to have lived.

OLIVER WENDELL HOLMES, JR.

I'd rather be a failure at something I love
than a success at something I hate.

GEORGE BURNS

$\mathcal{T}$RUTH

$\mathbf{R}$eality can be defined as the truth – the real nature of something – the facts. A key element to success is discovering and then facing reality – the reality of your opportunities, the reality of your corporate culture ... and more.

Choosing to search for the truth and having the courage to confront the hard realities will pay dividends to your career. You'll find the road to success a little straighter, the challenges less overwhelming and fewer surprises along the way.

Amid the frozen waters this cypress tree stands alone waiting for the dawn.
In life, we, too, may need to stand alone until the light comes.
Tom Fox

Reelfoot Lake State Park – Tennessee

Wisdom is choosing the purity of truth over popularity.

Face reality as it is … not as you wish it to be.

JACK WELCH

There is nothing so powerful as truth –
and often nothing so strange.

DANIEL WEBSTER

Accept everything about yourself – I mean everything. You are you
and that is the beginning and the end – no apologies, no regrets.

CLARK MOUSTAKAS

Tomorrow's greatest leaders are those with the courage to face reality
and help the people around them face reality.

RONALD HEIFETZ

I find the great thing in the world is not so much
where we stand, as in what direction we are standing.

GOETHE

Too many people overvalue what they are not and undervalue what they are.

MALCOLM FORBES

The golden opportunity you are seeking is in yourself. It is not in your environment;
it is not in luck or chance, or the help of others; it is in yourself alone.

ORISON SWETT MARDEN

When your heart speaks, take good notes.

ANONYMOUS

The truth is incontrovertible. Malice may attack it and
ignorance may deride it, but in the end, there it is.

WINSTON CHURCHILL

Truth has no special time of its own.
Its hour is now – always.

ALBERT SCHWEITZER

COURAGE

Courage is the inner drive to make progress regardless of the difficulty. For every person, there comes a time when you must step forward and meet the needs of the time. Regardless of whether your moment is now or sometime in the future, you must be ready.

When you move forward … even through the path of most resistance … you gain the courage necessary to win.

I photographed this compelling image just before sunset. The dramatic cloud pattern and sandstone swirls focus our attention on the rock pinnacle. This reminds me how important focus and perseverance are in achieving our goals.

TOM FOX

COLORADO PLATEAU

Courage is moving forward … even through the path of most resistance.

To see what is right and not to do it is cowardice.

CONFUCIUS

Courage is contagious. When a brave man takes a stand,
the spines of others are often stiffened.

BILLY GRAHAM

_With courage you will dare to take risks, have the strength to be compassionate
and the wisdom to be humble. Courage is the foundation of integrity._

KESHAVAN NAIR

_Courage is the first of human qualities because
it is the quality which guarantees all others._

WINSTON CHURCHILL

Whatever you do, you need courage.

RALPH WALDO EMERSON

We must build dikes of courage to hold back the flood of fear.

MARTIN LUTHER KING, JR.

He who loses wealth loses much; he who loses a friend loses more;

but he that loses his courage loses all.

MIGUEL DE CERVANTES

Man cannot discover new oceans
unless he has the courage to lose sight of the shore.

ANDRE GIDE

Courage is a special kind of knowledge; the knowledge of how to fear
what ought to be feared and how not to fear what ought not to be feared.

DAVID BEN-GURION

Courage changes things for the better ... With courage,
you can stay with something long enough to succeed at it –
realizing that it usually takes two, three, or four times
as long to succeed as you thought or hoped.

EARL NIGHTINGALE

$\mathcal{T}$EAMWORK

$\mathcal{W}$hat would life be without relationships?

Healthy relationships – those that are mutually caring and giving – are necessary for personal success. Everyone needs someone to learn from and share ideas. These relationships offer understanding when you fail, confidence when you're in doubt and celebration as you go through life. They also allow you opportunities to give, to mentor and to share.

Take time to nurture and appreciate the relationships that make a difference in your life.

As the morning sun brightened the canyon's red walls, I saw
the beautiful branch of silhouetted leaves suspended above me.
This image reminds me that everyone is unique but, inevitably, connected.

TOM FOX

PARIA CANYON – ARIZONA

Teamwork is connected independence.

Even the Lone Ranger didn't do it alone.

HARVEY MACKAY

Personal relationships are the fertile soil from which all advancement,
all success, all achievement in real life grows.

BEN STEIN

When nobody around you seems to measure up,
it's time to check your yardstick.

BILL LEMLEY

You will become like the five people you associate with the most.
This can be either a blessing or a curse.

BILLY COX

I believe that you can get everything in life you want
if you will just help enough other people get what they want.

ZIG ZIGLAR

It is surprising how much you can accomplish if you don't care who gets the credit.

ABRAHAM LINCOLN

One of the secrets of a long and fruitful life is to forgive everybody everything every night before going to bed.

BERNARD BARUCH

There is no exercise better for the heart
than reaching down and lifting people up.

JOHN ANDRES HOLMES

*Our rewards in life will always be in exact proportion
to the amount of consideration we show toward others.*

EARL NIGHTINGALE

*The golden rule is of no use whatsoever
unless you realize that it is your move.*

DR. FRANK CRANE

*Nice guys may appear to finish last,
but usually they are running in a different race.*

KEN BLANCHARD

THE VISION OF EXCELLENCE

True greatness consists in being great in little things.

CHARLES SIMMONS

VISION

Vision is a gift. It provides you the opportunity to clearly see how to expand your horizons and accomplish your goals.

Maintaining a laser-sharp focus on accomplishing goals is neither natural nor easy. Without question, you will face distractions that pull you away from your vision. That is okay as long as you quickly get back on track. Commit to your vision and be willing to pay the price to make your vision a reality.

This foggy country road is like the road of life. We may not be able to see
what lies ahead but, through faith, we can envision the unseen things beyond …
using the guideposts and distant landmarks to guide the way.

TOM FOX

GREAT SMOKY MOUNTAINS NATIONAL PARK — TENNESSEE

Vision is the gift to see what others only dream.

Where there is no vision, the people perish.

PROVERBS 29:18

Cherish your visions and your dreams as they are the children
of your soul; the blue prints of your ultimate achievements.

NAPOLEON HILL

You see things; and you say, "Why?"
But I dream things that never were; and I say, "Why not?"

GEORGE BERNARD SHAW

Vision looks inwards and becomes duty.
Vision looks outwards and becomes aspiration.
Vision looks upwards and becomes faith.

STEPHEN S. WISE

Vision without action is a daydream. Action without vision is a nightmare.

JAPANESE PROVERB

Only he who can see the invisible can do the impossible.

FRANK GAINES

We need to give ourselves permission to act
out our dreams and visions, not look for more sensations,
more phenomena, but live our strongest dreams –
even if it takes a lifetime.

VIJALI HAMILTON

The great thing in the world is not so much where
we stand, as in what direction we are moving.

OLIVER WENDELL HOLMES

*F*OCUS

The sun emits a billion kilowatts of energy per hour, yet we can deflect most of its harmful effects with an ultra-thin application of sunscreen or a visor, which diffuses its energy. On the other hand, a laser beam focuses only a few kilowatts of energy. Yet this relatively weak source of energy can cut a diamond in half or even eradicate certain types of cancer!

Laser-like clarity puts you on the fast track to excellence. The most important decision in life is to determine what is most important. Your time and energy are precious resources. Saying "Yes" to something by default means saying "No" to something else. So, focus your precious resources on what is most important to you.

This photograph was taken in a narrow slot canyon. As I looked up,
I focused on the sun's rays shining through a sandstone window.
Sorrow looks backward, worry looks around, but hope looks upward.

TOM FOX

ANTELOPE CANYON – ARIZONA

Stay focused. Discover what is most important … then stick to it.

focus

If you don't know where you are going, you will end up someplace else.

YOGI BERRA

Things that matter most must never be
at the mercy of things that matter least.

JOHANN WOLFGANG VON GOETHE

*I don't know the key to success, but the key
to failure is trying to please everybody.*

BILL COSBY

*Only one thing has to change for us to know happiness
in our lives: where we focus our attention.*

GREG ANDERSON

Be like a postage stamp. Stick to one thing until you get there.

JOSH BILLINGS

Most people have no idea of the giant capacity we can immediately command when we focus all of our resources on mastering a single area of our lives.

ANTHONY ROBBINS

The shortest way to do many things is to do only one thing at a time.

SYDNEY SMILES

If you surrender completely to the moments as they pass,
you live more richly those moments.

ANNE MORROW LINDBERGH

It is not good to have an oar in everyone's boat.

EARL CAMDEN

I try to learn from the past, but I plan for the future
by focusing exclusively on the present.
That's where the fun is.

DONALD TRUMP

$\mathcal{H}$OPE

Did you know that the bumblebee should *not* be able to fly? Based on its size, weight and shape of its body in relationship to the total wing span, a flying bumblebee is aerodynamically impossible.

The bumblebee, being ignorant of scientific data, goes ahead and flies anyway, making honey every day.

Ignore the sting of the past and replace it with hope for a brighter future. If you do, you will be able to achieve things everyone else thinks are impossible. Keep your hopes high and you will fly to new heights!

From their protected cliff dwelling, these ancient Anasazi ruins overlook the sunlit mesas below. This inspirational view is reminiscent of looking from the shadows of the past to the hope of the future.

TOM FOX

CANYONLANDS NATIONAL PARK — UTAH

The past does not have a future, but you do.

hope

For the hopes of men have been justly called waking dreams.

SAINT BASIL

Do not follow where the path may lead.
Go, instead, where there is no path and leave a trail.

UNKNOWN

Learn from yesterday, live for today and hope for tomorrow.
The important thing is not to stop questioning.

ALBERT EINSTEIN

Most of the important things in the world have been accomplished by people
who have kept on trying when there seemed to be no hope at all.

DALE CARNEGIE

The present is the ever moving shadow that divides
yesterday from tomorrow. In that lies hope.

FRANK LLOYD WRIGHT

In times of change, there is no incentive so great,
and no medicine so powerful as the hope for a better tomorrow.

UNKNOWN

Our greatest good, and what we least can spare, is hope:
the last of all our evils, fear.

JOHN ARMSTRONG

The grand essentials to happiness in this life are something to do,
something to love, and something to hope for.

JOSEPH ADDISON

Some of the world's greatest feats were accomplished by people
not smart enough to know they were impossible.

UNKNOWN

Don't dwell on what went wrong. Instead, focus on what to do next.
Spend your energies on moving forward toward finding the answer.

DENIS WAITLEY

$\mathcal{D}$REAMS

$\mathcal{N}$ever, ever stop dreaming. If you follow the trail to your dreams, your dreams can become your reality. Keep moving forward and avoid the roadblocks that prevent you from accomplishing your dreams.

Dreams are to be lived out … wake up and begin living your dream today!

Some trails have unexpected rewards. After many years of hiking and photographing, I've found the most fulfillment in following less-traveled paths to the lesser-known destinations.

TOM FOX

BIG SOUTH FORK PARK — TENNESSEE

Follow the trail to your dreams, not the path of others' expectations.

dreams

Dream no small dreams for they have no power to move the hearts of men.

JOHANN WOLFGANG VON GOETHE

When you cease to dream you cease to live.

MALCOLM S. FORBES

I'll do my dreaming with my eyes wide open,
and I'll do my looking back with my eyes closed.

TONY ARATA

Nothing is as real as a dream.
The world can change around you, but your dream will not.
Responsibilities need not erase it. Duties need not obscure it.
Because the dream is within you, no one can take it away.

TOM CLANCY

Don't ever let anyone steal your dreams.

DEXTER YAGER

Dream lofty dreams, and as you dream, so shall you become.

JOHN RUSKIN

I have heard it said that the first ingredient of success –
the earliest spark in the dreaming youth – is this:
dream a great dream.

JOHN ALAN APPLEMAN

We've got to have a dream
if we are going to make a dream come true.

DENIS E. WAITLEY

Make every thought, every fact, that comes into your mind
pay you a profit. Make it work and produce for you.
Think of things not as they are but as they might be.
Don't merely dream – but create!

ROBERT COLLIER

Aim at heaven and you get earth thrown in;
aim at earth and you get neither.

C.S. LEWIS

MAKE THE DIFFERENCE

We all know people who have intentions of making a difference. It could be helping a neighbor, mentoring a young person, volunteering to coach or providing transportation for those in need.

Intentions do not accomplish anything. Eventually you have to decide to step out and make a difference. It could begin today. It could begin right now. For a better tomorrow, step out and make a difference today!

One morning while snowshoeing and searching for the route to take,
I photographed this majestic scene. I remembered the promise,
"Trust in the Lord … and He will direct your paths."

TOM FOX

SOUTHWESTERN COLORADO

Step out ... make the difference.

make the difference

If you think you're too small to have an impact,
try going to bed with a mosquito in the room.

DAME ANITA RODDICK

Opportunities multiply as they are seized.

JOHN WICKER

Don't wait. The time will never be just right. Start where you stand and work with whatever
tools you may have at your command and better tools will be found as you go along.

NAPOLEON HILL

Why not go out on a limb? That's where the fruit is.

WILL ROGERS

Seize every moment and passionately pursue life by being
the very best you can be. No looking back. No regrets!

KEN CARNES

One of the marks of successful people is that they are action-oriented.
One of the marks of average people is that they are talk-oriented.

BRIAN TRACY

Take a chance! All life is a chance.
The man who goes the furthest is generally the one who is willing
to do a dare. The "sure thing" boat never gets far from shore.

DALE CARNEGIE

Having the world's best idea will do you no good unless you act on it.
People who want milk shouldn't sit on a stool in the middle of a field
in hopes that a cow will back up to them.

CURTIS GRANT

Everyone who has ever taken a shower has an idea.
It's the person who gets out of the shower, dries off and
does something about it who makes a difference.

NOLAN BUSHNELL

REFLECTION

Just as water reflects your image as you gaze into it, when you look inside yourself, you see who you really are. Your knowledge and success with others is directly related to your self-knowledge.

Excellence is built from the inside out. Therefore, reflect on who you are, what you can be and where you are going. Your reflection paints your vision for excellence.

I discovered this compelling scene in a remote desert location.
The radiant evergreen tree exemplifies the resolute determination
to succeed even in a rocky barren environment.

TOM FOX

COLORADO PLATEAU

Success is a reflection of your commitment to excellence.

reflection

Knowledge of the self is the mother of all knowledge.
So it is incumbent on me to know my self, to know it completely.

KAHLIL GIBRAN

The unexamined life is not worth living.

SOCRATES

Nature is the greatest teacher and
I learn from her best when others are asleep.

GEORGE WASHINGTON CARVER

Two things fill the heart with renewed and increasing awe and reverence,
the more often and the more steadily that they are meditated on:
the starry skies above me and the moral law inside me.

IMMANUEL KANT

Before anything else, preparation is the key to success.

ALEXANDER GRAHAM BELL

He that knows himself, knows others.

CHARLES CALEB COLTON

*The outward freedom that we shall attain will only be in exact proportion
to the inward freedom to which we may have grown at a given moment.
And if this is a correct view of freedom, our chief energy
must be concentrated on achieving reform from within.*

GANDHI

Blessed are those who can laugh at themselves,
for they shall never cease to be amused.

ANONYMOUS

*Don't bother just to be better than your contemporaries
or predecessors. Try to be better than yourself.*

WILLIAM FAULKNER

It's not the plan that is important, it's the planning.

GRAEME EDWARDS

THE ACTS OF EXCELLENCE

A man is the sum of his actions, of what he has done, of what he can do. Nothing else.

MAHATMA GANDHI

ATTITUDE

GROWTH

PRESS ON

CHANGE

PATIENCE

PERSEVERANCE

$\mathscr{A}$TTITUDE

Your attitude toward life is the most important choice you make. Your attitude reflects your past, describes your present and predicts your future.

The great news is that even in the worst situations – a victim of a natural disaster, prisoner of war, target of abuse or when hit by a string of unfortunate circumstances – your attitude is something you can always control. You are the conductor of your own attitude! Nobody else can compose your thoughts for you.

The pursuit of excellence requires you to control your own attitude. If you do, you will create a powerful ripple effect that can have a positive impact many people and miles away. Your attitude is your personal boomerang to the world – whatever you throw out will come back to you. Receive tomorrow what you give today.

I walked into this foggy field and marveled at the sunlit tree standing with a smaller tree in the background. The two trees appeared to sustain one another even though they were yards apart. This photograph reminds me that my attitude should be supportive of others, even when separated.

TOM FOX

GREAT SMOKY MOUNTAINS NATIONAL PARK – TENNESSEE

The right attitude is the root to success. It enables us to stand strong and prevail.

The greatest discovery of my generation is that human beings can alter their lives by altering their attitudes of mind.

WILLIAM JAMES

An optimist sees an opportunity in every calamity;
a pessimist a calamity in every opportunity.

WINSTON CHURCHILL

If you want to be happy, put your effort into controlling the sail, not the wind.

ANONYMOUS

There's very little difference in people. But that little difference makes a big difference. The little difference is attitude. The BIG DIFFERENCE is whether it is positive or negative.

W. CLEMENT STONE

Ask yourself a question: Is my attitude worth catching?

ZIG ZIGLAR

Think enthusiastically about everything; but especially about your job.
If you do so, you'll put a touch of glory in your life. If you love your job
with enthusiasm, you'll shake it to pieces.

NORMAN VINCENT PEALE

Every man is enthusiastic at times. One man has enthusiasm for thirty minutes,
another man has it for thirty days. But it is the man who has it
for thirty years who makes a success in life.

EDWARD B. BUTLER

Years may wrinkle the skin,
but to give up enthusiasm wrinkles the soul.

SAMUEL ULLMAN

Everything can be taken from a person but one thing:
the last of human freedoms – to choose one's attitude in
any given set of circumstances, to choose one's own way.

VIKTOR E. FRANKL

Life is too short not to be happy and too long not to do well.

BRYAN DODGE

GROWTH

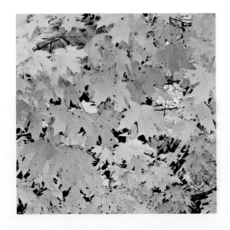

Trees grow up through their branches, down through their roots and grow wider with each passing year. As growth occurs, trees eventually shed their protective bark to make way for growth. Humans are the same way.

Just as trees need bark as a protective shield while growth occurs, you need boundaries to defend your vulnerabilities as your potential unfolds … but your ongoing growth depends on your ability to shed this "bark" of protection when it is no longer needed. In some cases, an inability to shed this bark will constrict your ability to realize your full potential.

But unlike trees, which shed their bark automatically, you must consciously adjust your comfort zones. Create the mental space you need to learn new skills, to stretch your thinking, to deepen your emotions … and to grow!

This tree's magnificent fall foliage represents another year of completed growth.
Then, reluctantly, it lets go of its leaves in preparation for the new growth of spring.
TOM FOX

LAGRANGE, TENNESSEE

You must let go to grow.

Thought, not money, is the real business capital.

HARVEY S. FIRESTONE

Growth begins when we start to accept our own weakness.

JEAN VANIER

He who rejects change is the architect of decay.

HAROLD WILSON

Learning without thought is labor lost;
thought without learning is perilous.

CONFUCIUS

Conformity is the jailer of freedom
and the enemy of growth.

JOHN F. KENNEDY

The man who graduates today and stops learning tomorrow
is uneducated the day after.

NEWTON D. BAKER

Perfection does not exist – you can always do better
and you can always grow.

LES BROWN

In teaching others, we teach ourselves.

PROVERB

What we have to learn to do, we learn by doing.

ARISTOTLE

Learning is a treasure that will follow its owner everywhere.

CHINESE PROVERB

$\mathscr{P}$RESS ON

At one time or another, all of us are confronted by adversity. The question you have to answer is, "How am I going to respond to the adversity I am facing?" Many times, adversity provides you the opportunity to explore new thoughts, ideas and solutions you, otherwise, may not have considered.

Whatever situation you are facing, press on with the presence of mind to explore workable alternatives so you can overcome the adversity and move upward to the next level.

I carefully walked out onto the frozen lake before sunrise to photograph this unusual scene. The ice was frozen in a unique tile-like pattern and splashed up on the cypress tree trunks. As the sun rose, it was truly an incredible experience.

Tom Fox

Reelfoot Lake State Park – Tennessee

Press on. Your defining moment may arrive just when you feel surrounded by adversity.

press on

Within all of us are wells of thought and dynamos of energy which are not suspected until emergencies arise. Then, oftentimes, we find that it is comparatively simple to double or triple our former capacities and to amaze ourselves by the results achieved.

THOMAS J. WATSON

Adversity introduces a man to himself.

ANONYMOUS

We are continually faced with great opportunities brilliantly disguised as insolvable problems.

LEE IACOCCA

Adversity causes some men to break, others to break records.

WILLIAM ARTHUR WARD

This, too, shall pass.

WILLIAM SHAKESPEARE

*The very greatest things – great thoughts, discoveries, inventions –
have usually been nurtured in hardship, often pondered over in sorrow,
and at length established with difficulty.*

SAMUEL SMILES

*Life is a series of experiences, each one of which makes us bigger,
even though sometimes it is hard to realize this. For the world was built to develop character,
and we must learn that the setbacks and griefs which we endure help us in our marching onward.*

HENRY FORD

The measure of a man is not where he stands in moments of convenience,
but where he stands in times of challenge and adversity.

DR. MARTIN LUTHER KING

Trouble is opportunity in work clothes.

W. CLEMENT STONE

*Things don't go wrong and break your heart so you can become bitter
and give up. They happen to break you down and build you up
so you can be all that you were intended to be.*

CHARLIE "TREMENDOUS" JONES

CHANGE

Change is inevitable … and it happens fast! It takes more energy to resist change than it does to embrace it. Change is like rain. Everyone knows it's good for us, but nobody wants to get wet.

Your resistance to change is rooted in the fear of the unknown. Therefore, you gain great power and confidence by understanding what a particular change means to you. As you understand change and your reactions to it, you begin to see the growth and benefits that change can bring. You may never use an umbrella again!

I saw this beautiful waterfall during a very difficult canyon hike.
The water was reflecting the sunlit walls above, while the shadowed canyon cast the bluish color.
These colors changed the water into something magical.

TOM FOX

ZION NATIONAL PARK – UTAH

Change the way you look at things, and things will change the way they look.

If you never change your mind, why have one?

EDWARD DE BONO

We cannot become what we need to be
by remaining what we are.

MAX DEPREE

Never doubt that a small group of concerned citizens can change the world.
Indeed, it is the only thing that ever has.

MARGARET MEAD

The only person who is educated is the one
who has learned how to learn … and change.

CARL ROGERS

Change your thoughts and you change your world.

NORMAN VINCENT PEALE

When you blame others, you give up your power to change.

ANONYMOUS

I used to say, "I sure hope things will change."
Then I learned that the only way things are going
to change for me is when I change.

JIM ROHN

If we don't change, we don't grow.
If we don't grow, we aren't really living.

GAIL SHEEHY

Who we are never changes. Who we think we are does.

MARY S. ALMANAC

If you focus on results, you will never change.
If you focus on change, you will get results.

JACK DIXON

$\mathscr{P}$ATIENCE

$\mathbf{T}$he rewards of patience are similar to the results of planting an exotic Chinese bamboo seed. When this particular seed is planted and nurtured, it can take up to two years for a sprout to break through the earth. It requires the right watering, sunlight, care and feeding so it can build a strong root structure and foundation for growth, none of which is visible above ground. However, once it breaks ground, this plant can grow over 100 feet in two weeks! The benefits of patience are abundant with this seed … just as they are with personal patience.

Be impatient to plant the seeds of excellence, but be patient enough to watch them grow.

These giant evergreen trees towered over an array of delicate wild flowers.
However, the trees needed years of growth to achieve their greatness.
Likewise, we must be willing to grow patiently in life.

TOM FOX

GREAT SMOKY MOUNTAINS NATIONAL PARK – TENNESSEE

Greatness takes time to grow.

A handful of patience is worth more than a bushel of brains.

DANISH PROVERB

Our patience will achieve more than our force.

EDMUND BURKE

You can chase a butterfly all over the field and never catch it.
But if you sit quietly in the grass, it will come and sit on your shoulder.

ANONYMOUS

Beware of undertaking too much at the start. Be content with quite a little.
Allow for accidents. Allow for human nature, especially your own.

ARNOLD BENNETT

Patience makes lighter what sorrow may not heal.

HORACE

Patience is something you admire in the driver behind you,
but not in one ahead.

BILL MCGLASHEN

The sea does not reward those who are too anxious, too greedy, or too impatient.
To dig for treasures shows not only impatience and greed, but lack of faith.
Patience, patience, patience, is what the sea teaches. Patience and faith.
One should lie empty, open, choiceless as a beach – waiting for a gift from the sea.

ANNE MORROW LINDBERGH

Patience is also a form of action.

AUGUSTE RODIN

The strongest of all warriors are these two –
Time and Patience.

LEO TOLSTOY

Take it slow like a pro.

RONALD H. DAVIS

$\mathscr{P}$ERSEVERANCE

The signature of mediocrity is constantly changing direction. The signature of excellence is sticking to it. Excellence does not depend upon the brilliance of your plan, but upon the consistency of your actions.

A good plan gets you into the race, but sticking to it gets you into the winner's circle. Life offers plenty of excuses to quit the race, but excellence is achieved by those who let their actions rise above their excuses. Win or lose … you choose. Stick to it and win!

I saw this beautiful yucca plant, glowing in the sunlight as a storm approached.
The yucca's deep roots allow it to survive, and even thrive, in a difficult environment.
We can do the same thing – if we develop deep roots.

TOM FOX

WHITE SANDS NATIONAL MONUMENT – NEW MEXICO

Against all odds, persevere.

perseverance

Genius? Nothing! Sticking to it is the genius! …
I've failed my way to success.

THOMAS EDISON

The secret to success is constancy of purpose.

BENJAMIN DISRAELI

The major difference between the big shot and the little shot
is the big shot is just a little shot who kept on shooting.

ZIG ZIGLAR

The difference between perseverance and obstinacy is that one
often comes from a strong will, and the other from a strong won't.

HENRY WARD BEECHER

Don't judge each day by the harvest you reap,
but by the seeds you plant.

ROBERT LOUIS STEVENSON

Don't quit before the blessing.

BYRD BAGGETT

*When one door closes another door opens; but we often look so long and so regretfully
upon the closed door that we do not see the ones which open for us.*

ALEXANDER GRAHAM BELL

Persistent people begin their success
where others end in failure.

EDWARD EGGLESTON

Nothing in the world can take the place of persistence.

Talent will not; nothing is more common than unsuccessful men with talent.

Genius will not; unrewarded genius is almost a proverb.

Education will not; the world is full of educated derelicts.

Persistence and determination alone are omnipotent.

CALVIN COOLIDGE

There are no traffic jams along the extra mile.

ROGER STAUBACH

THE *Essence*
OF *Excellence*

Excellent people have excellent habits. They sacrifice today's pleasures for tomorrow's rewards. You don't compete for excellence against others, but you do compete against your own potential every day. It's not a destination – it's a mindset you take on your journey.

You don't have to be excellent to get started, but you do have to get started to be excellent.

The sun was setting behind the mountains' silhouette
when I made this inspirational and reflective image.
As in water, face reflects face ... so in life, excellence reflects excellence.

TOM FOX

SOUTHWESTERN COLORADO

Excellence is reflected in each of us.

Use what talents you possess; the woods would be very silent
if no birds sang there except those that sang best.

HENRY VAN DYKE

Good enough never is.

DEBBI FIELD

Excellence is the result of caring more than others think is wise,
risking more than others think is safe, dreaming more than others
think is practical, and expecting more than others think is possible.

ANONYMOUS

Excellence is in the details.
Give attention to the details and excellence will come.

PERRY PAXTON

Excellence is doing ordinary things extraordinarily well.

JOHN W. GARDNER

The quality of a person's life is in direct proportion to their commitment
to excellence, regardless of their chosen field of endeavor.

VINCE LOMBARDI

To aim at excellence, our reputation, and friends, and all must be ventured;
to aim at the average we run no risk and provide little service.

OLIVER GOLDSMITH

When you were born, you cried and the world rejoiced.
Live your life in such a manner that when you die
the world cries and you rejoice.

OLD INDIAN SAYING

People forget how fast you did a job,
but they remember how well you did it.

HOWARD W. NEWTON

Always do your best.
What you plant now, you will harvest later.

OG MANDINO

We hope you enjoyed ***The Nature of Excellence*** and that it has inspired you to pursue excellence in every endeavor.

All photographs in this book are available as fine art prints.
Visit **www.TomFoxPhotography.com** or call 901-753-8252.

Watch a three-minute inspirational video featuring the words and images from ***The Nature of Excellence*** at **www.CornerStoneLeadership.com**.

Most of the photographs featured in this book are available as inspirational note cards, posters and desktop prints. Customized gift versions of this book are also available.

Visit **www.CornerStoneLeadership.com** or call 888-789-5323.

Best wishes in your pursuit of excellence!